NDN:
The words of a little hawk

NDN:
The words of a little hawk

poems by
Elaine Gerard

Poetic Justice Books & Arts
Port Saint Lucie, Florida

©2019 Elaine Gerard

book design and layout: SpiNDec, Port Saint Lucie, FL
photography and artwork: Elaine Gerard
cover design: Kevin Cline

All rights reserved.

No part of this book may be used or reproduced in any manner whatsoever without written permission except in the case of brief quotations embodied in critical articles and reviews. Members of educational institutions and organizations wishing to photocopy any of the work for classroom use, or authors, artists and publishers who would like to obtain permission for any material in the work, should contact the publisher.

Published by Poetic Justice Books
Port Saint Lucie, Florida
www.poeticjusticebooks.com

ISBN: 978-1-950433-17-9

FIRST EDITION
10 9 8 7 6 5 4 3 2 1

NDN:
The words of a little hawk

Dedication ix

Forward xi

Prologue 3
Sugar for My Soul

Childhood Short and Sweet 7
My Magic Shoes
Father's Gift
My Mother's Song
A Simple Thing

On Being NDN 21
Don't Eat the Snow
My Uncivil Heart
Paying the Cultural Rent
Make Them Look

Montana in My Blood 35
Reading Tracks
Blue Horses
Listen to the Voices in the Wind
Sleepy Highway
Something Ran Across the Road

Peering Into the Cracked Mirror of a Marriage 49
Nizhoni-Oh
Desert Rain

Just Stop It
You Shouldn't Have
A Man in a Grave

Divorce/Poverty 61
Burnt Weenies and Honey
Ejaculation Nation
A Free Love
Making a Fist

Sex and Lies I Tell Myself 75
Furry Cup of Redemption
Hues
In the Jungle of Your Mind
Laundromat Thoughts

Need 87
Writing My List
For All the Rocks
My Cup
Sleeping Alone

Who Am I? What Am I? 99
Grendel's Bride
Heyah
Mistaken Beauty
The Human in Me
One Legged Bird
Searching for Kind Elaine

Healing, Moving Ahead 119
Letting Go
My Comfort Zone
Remembering to Forget
The Fiber of a Day

Coming Home to You 131
A Note Left Under Your Pillow
Nightmare Repairs
The Usual Path

This Is How It Began, This Is How It Ends 139
Sugar for My Soul

about the author 143
acknowledgements 145

Dedication

For Kevin, you are my cosmic twin, may we ever continue to make noise, art and music and to love and live together until death do us part.

For Erin and Rose, my children, may these words give you guidance and hope. We aren't given all the answers in life but we can do this one thing. Be proud of who you are and let your NDN blood show you the way.

For my sisters and brothers, we all forge on as one.

For my big Facebook family, you have been the wind under my shaky wings.

For Mom and Dad, for bringing so many wonderful human beings onto this planet.

*For my Creator, for all You give us, for setting the stars in motion, for rolling this ball of dirt into a worthy planet, for breathing life into a lump of clay and calling it a man. For setting fruit in the trees, food in the ground, a rainbow in the sky as a sign of your covenant with mankind.
Thank you.*

Forward

"Crossing all boundaries, Elaine Gerard's writing style is powerful. She draws the reader into the moment. As you read, you can smell the words. You can wrap the words and give voice to the wordless ideas. Direct and deceptively simple, she takes layers of complex emotion into the human psyche. When you come to the core of a poem, it makes your soul stand still, for a moment, and open its eyes to a different world."

M.S. McCloskey

NDN:
The words of a little hawk

Prologue

This is how it goes. Life spits out a silent little girl who watches the world, a beleaguered teen into the mean streets and a married woman out the door of life as a divorcee. She is finding her way. She writes a simple little poem one day that fans a spark for a fire that she once thought died decades ago.

I wrote a poem.

Circa 2006

Sugar for My Soul

*Is what I really need
In my own two hands?
Can I learn to look in the mirror
And to walk out the door strong
like a man?*

*I don't want to peek around corners
For the rest of my life
I don't want to be nice all the time
But I will have a cup of tea
Every single day
And I will take two lumps
of sugar for my soul.*

Childhood, Short and Sweet

Little girls fall down and skin their knees. Then they go and hide because no one should ever bleed like that, no one should ever hurt.

My Magic Shoes

A long time ago,
out on the Montana prairie,
in those days when nothing
grew between the phone poles
but desolate prairie grass,
yellow wheat stubble and
endless banks of snow,
a little brown girl
began to grow hair,
she also grew toenails
and this attitude,
but that's another story.
This little brown girl
had holes in her shoes
and holes in the knees
of her hand-me-downs;
no matter, because
those shoes were a
shiny gift from the
almighty god of
JC Penney,
and she knows
that she is as beautiful
and desirable as wind
and snow and rain
in desolate prairie coulees
and ridge lines where
hawks fly off of updrafts
of the thermal laws of air,
and where the bones of
buffalo settle in the silence.

She knows that those shoes
are her ticket to something,
what, she is not sure of,
but as she walks to school
in the snow, she looks behind
and behold! beautiful red roses
are blossoming in each little
footprint in cold Montana winter
and she shivers and embraces
the cold sharp pain and
reaches down to tuck
another piece of fresh cardboard
into her shoes to cover the holes
and continues her journey,
leaving her ordinary destiny
in the bloody footprints
left behind.

Father's Gift

There is a scream caught
in my throat
that wants to carry
anger, despair
raining down
on the father
that left us
over and over,
the brown faces
of children waiting,
car in the driveway,
footsteps and arms
that loved us
and lifted us
above the ordinary,
validated our little
brown mouse existence
in a Lutheran princess
fairyland town
and gave our ordinary
brown Indian faces
shiny hope and wings to soar
above privileged daughters
of bankers and lawyers
as beloved children,
children with a father,
protected little ones
in this enemy's camp.

You are long gone, father,
and we have wandered away

to find our own strengths,
our wit our only weapon
in this enemy's world,
and a gift that you gave us
in leaving us behind
was the warrior soul,
the drumbeat of our
leather Indian hearts
reflected off brown skin,
shining brown eyes,
and the strong arms
that lift our weapons
to life in this battle,
fatherless children,
warriors of your blood,
defenders of your memory.

My Mother's Song

A lonely wind leaps
over Heart Butte,
moaning low, wandering
along gentle waters
to finally lie down quiet,
tucked into Sweetgrass Hills,
nestled in with the
dreams of long gone
men and women
with brown faces
lined by their sorrow
and hardships,
the smiles borne along
by friendship and love,
and hearts that soared
to an eagle's high whistle.

My mother rides a lone horse
across a somber yellow prairie,
purple lupines bow to her
as she passes quietly,
the grass swooshes,
her canteen clinking along
to the soft hooves of her
gentle dun mare,
as she travels with her thoughts.

Her name is Rides a Yellow Horse,
as if she were a funny little antelope
that runs and leaps in the spring,
that tastes like tough sagebrush

with bright eyes that see far away
the vistas of blue mountains,
wavering in the summer heat,
grasshoppers rattle and fuss,
a lonely twee of a prairie bird,
flicker of color and flash of light,
the quiet jangle of a bridle
and the rhythmic squeak of
her well-worn saddle leather.

She stops on her way into woods,
looks back east on the prairie,
its endless wavering sea of grasses,
alive and crawling across her mind,
drinks from her cold canteen,
the creek water trickling sweet
down into her dry silent soul,
and she loves the emptiness of it all,
the loneliness of independence and her
horse spirit heart that calls to no one but her.

From far away she sees a bird on wing,
it circles lazily above then comes to her,
alights on her saddle horn and then
arches its proud brown head to
her gentle caress from a gloved hand,
the eagle lowers its head to her touch,
watches her fondly with fierce yellow eyes,
and then, they ride on together,

my mother and the golden eagle.

The day is drawn down into darkness,
I am sleepless here in this city,
restless for no reason other than
the blood that boils in my soul,
the blood of my mother that pounds
with the sounds of wild horses' hooves,
and a voice that sings with the eagles,
I feel a fight coming on, I feel fierce,
I feel my mother's song rising up,
prairie yellow bird and dun mare song,
the songs of long gone ancestors,
their fierce faces and large noses,
sharp spears and arrows
pointed straight up to the heavens,
strung with feathers of a thousand
golden eagles and the teeth of
a thousand bears and wolves,
and I open my voice and sing
on this cold quiet city night,
where windows fly open and
dogs that barked long in the night
now become silent,
as they all stop
and listen
to my mother's song.

A Simple Thing

Sequestered in dust balls,
I am under the bed
breathing in the sweet silence,
it's where I feel safe,
where I think such clear blue sky
and radiant lavender thoughts,
there is nobody else here
and the quiet house
hums to itself
on a sunny long gone day.

It is summer 1963
and I am lying on
a mowed lawn.
The blades of grass are monstrous
as I lie on my belly half asleep,
watch ants hurry
in and out of their hole,
each grasps one grain of dirt
and after much indecision and
fussing about, the grain is deposited
neatly and solidly in its appointed place.

I envy the little ants their communal life,
they waggle antennae excitedly
and seem to be passing busy thoughts.
They stay together on their paths and
fight invaders with loyalty and unity,
where I seek only my solitude,
sucking on a straw and listening
to a cricket chirruping in the garage,

idly pulling the wings off flies
and feeding them to grateful spiders.

Perhaps I should have been a bug,
been able to let my feelings known
by mere touch of antennae or
perhaps invisible rays of message
flowing from one to another,
for this is something I don't
or can't do here with this
big nested anthill of humanity,
where big talk and big words rule,
and the heavy hammer of the fist
is what we all bow down to,
bloody nose and black eye,
I learn to watch the floor.

The night swirls in
and I climb out from under the bed.
The family has arrived home.
As they flow into the house
talking and jostling,
stepping on toes and pushing,
I stand to the side and watch.
I was always watching.
That is what I do,
but in the closing of eyes
in beds with squirming bed partners,
sisters and brothers whispering in the dark,
I watch the sentient ceiling

and return to antennae moments.
It is then I wonder,
what is the mystery of me,
why am I afraid and
why do I always wish to be alone?

On Being Indian

Nobody would choose this path in life, to be this anomaly, this human being who has been born into a vanquished invisible forgotten people. But this human being did, and we all rise up from where we were and become something beautiful and proud and thriving.

Don't Eat the Snow

I will drop to my knees
Before the mighty snowbank
Watching the turquoise milk
That pours from her teat,
The ice cold blue that
Ripples and sings,
I will lick the chaff and bone dust
Of all those who died here,
The fallen brown skinned women,
Stoic and now silent,
The dirty snow holds them all;
For Siokskitis, Charcoal, the kind man,
whose spirit roams these mountains,
His soul captured in a still moment
As he stopped and looked back,
A mountain breeze that took it
And stole it back to the memories,
The stories of his life,
Dripping from his arms as mythology,
Smoke and sage scented fringe,
Like the white ermine skins that
Drape each shoulder, white like
The dirty snow that holds us all,
The bones and dust of our own,
That blanket this northern land,
Whispering out of pine boughs
That wave and caress the winds,
And the white blankets of snow
That I bow and begin to eat,
Each memory painted in sepia tint,
Sliding down my 20th century throat,

It tastes like the meat of a thousand
Slaughtered bison hung out to dry,
Landfill for the mighty machine,
Like an ocean roaring and churning
With a million salmon flashing red,
The hooves of a rainbow full of horses,
And the stride of moccasin'ed feet marching
And disappearing into the brown earth,
Resolute and calm, those watching eyes,
The march down my throat, into my soul,
Invading every corpuscle, every corner,
Down to DNA, the only reason for my being,
The reason I have these little hands balled
Into fists full of purpose and intent,
The reason my eyes are fierce and discontent
As I watch the seasons roll and wave and ebb,
Across the ocean of pale blue sky,
The reason why I will always fight,
My only reason for living.

My Uncivil Heart

Save me from this burning world;
I don't want to be this scorched woman.
My soul is fading away into dust,
the heart that pounded has grown quiet
in my chest where I cradled my children,
long gone away to their destinies
with their love and their energy
dissipated into the lonely wind
that chatters around the corners of
the graveyard of a family
nearly forgotten, that bitter taste,
the coffee grounds memory,
the bloody shoe, the taste of salty tears
grown into such translucency.

We live in square chunks
of time, of memory,
carved up neatly,
dying spaces left behind,
page after calendar page,
fluttering away.
I want my children's children
to take me to my rest,
there in the silent prairie,
whispering its secrets
into ancient ears.
I want to be a warrior
and greet my Master
with pride,
I want to be his soldier
and ride into that

good place.

I will allow myself to bleed
into brown dirt, there in that sleep,
for I am Indian bred and born.
My endeavor of civilized effort
finds this such a hard place to be,
here in this cubical world
where lines and whistles
put me in my place,
but I look away
and I see out of the corner
of slatted dark eyes,
the tattered edge of an arrow
and the shaggy heart
of the Indian beast
that wishes to rival
the best efforts of
your teacup world.

So matrons of the white world,
grace us all with your airs
and watch me lift a cup
with grace and wit to match yours,
but know this,
that when the war cry comes,
I will drop my pretty cup
and race to my truth,
the bitter war will end,

I will emerge
uncivilized woman,
my battle over,
and my leather Indian heart
embraced.

"The civilized man has built a coach,
but has lost the use of his feet."
Ralph Waldo Emerson

Paying the Cultural Rent

I'm not your pretty little Indian;
keep your hands off me
or lose it.
I took down the fence
not so long ago,
and I'm running free
trample and steam ahead,
hurt and maim,
love and hate,
kiss and slap.

I like the sound of a
bow being drawn;
I like seeing you
sighted down that shaft,
and when I let go,
the arrow
will flee from my hand
to your already
wounded soul,
pierced through
and dropped.

Where does an Indian woman's
soul lie down?
Where is my prairie dawn
and the smoke of
the sweet grass,
which climbs to heaven,
while I wait down here
in this precious dirt,

my leather strap
around your neck?

Don't put a teacup on my lap,
I will spill its precious contents
and throw it on the ground,
while I try to read the tea leaves
and see what I can there,
in its brown message,
my brown message,
the water that flows down,
the blood that boils in me,
the Indian blood that
demands revenge,
a native woman's fierce nature
that possesses no correctness
in your culture,
the ugly Indian woman's face,
the drunken Indian woman
on the corner,
native grandmother who needs
no one and nothing
but the sound of a prairie wind
and the pure odor of the
sweet grass as it carries
my soul away to its waiting.

Make Them Look

The old man lay
bent and twisted
in the snow,
there is silence
all around,
for his survivors
who gather their
leather and
their children
and they go away
into a new prison,
a cultural cage
that said NO
at every turn,
a cultural cage
that said no more.

His horse died too
that day,
an Indian horse
with shagged mane
hooves run ragged
onto prairie dirt,
where no bird sang
and no man or woman
prayed.
The soldiers gather them
and lay them in a hole,
stand proud and tall
for their picture,
then they bury the dead.

We are arisen from
that frozen grave,
we are taking it back,
and in breaking out
of this cultural cage,
we now say NO,
we now say
no more.

Montana in My Blood

Sometimes, being born in a harsh beautiful place can lodge itself in the deep inner recesses of the brain. And when your ancestors' bones and blood are planted in that dirt, it will never leave. It is your DNA.

Reading Tracks

There is a rare time
Of looking back
At what was left,
Behind the broken
Bushes and bales,
The sideways kiss,
The slap and fall.
Sometimes I just run
Into the next day
And hope shadows
Won't follow me,
That dreams will
Carry me away
Into escape,
That the smell
Of ease and charm
That you left on me
Will fade into bloody
And purpling sunrise.
There are tracks
Leading away now,
They circle me,
Circumventing and
Leaving behind a
Witness, lightness
Of existence,
Of ownership
Of lies.
They whisper and then
Bark at gentle moonlight,
Taking away my ache.

They startle me in the dark
Then tease me at daybreak,
The Montana sky
Sliding deeply into midnight,
Soft ground alive with crawling
And creeping life,
Surviving the bitter cold,
Stranded by cruel summer
Who left us here so hungry,
Those of us who seek out
That thing, that food,
That startling need.
We search the night,
Lick the snow and
Then stop to glare
Upon the cold cold moon
As it raises its ashen face
Watches those of us here.
We turn to leave our
Footprints in the snow,
And our blood
In the tracks.

Blue Horses

Sun shines through
a veil of blue cloud,
coy and hesitant
to warm the hides
of tired cold horses,
I watch them cross
a yellow line,
stop, lower heads,
eat then move on.
I see the clouds
watching and waiting,
a bird clutching
a hank of wind
rolls into view,
gains control and
disappears into grass.
I sip this cold tea
and dream about
things I should not,
about the things
I barely remember,
the things I forgot
and I think about
the things I should
have done.
I look to the north
for more winter,
the dark blue line
that heralds snow,
the cold breath of
mighty old man winter.

I shiver and watch
the rolling yellow grass
and boiling dirty snow
as it spills around corners
and across roadways,
drifting and piling,
restless and infinite,
maddening, relentless.
The house shudders
as if it too feels so cold
that it wants to shake off
the dirty snow that
clings to thick hide, fur,
and run away to warmth,
summer with its greenness
and stinging armies of flies,
always another season,
another reason to run,
to shake and to kick,
another day in the sun.
So here I sit,
the snow boils over,
the horses stop
to hang heads,
the bird hides
and the wind
sings a song,
a blue song
of horses.

Listen to the Voices in the Wind

I know it is cold out,
and winter is breathing
her frosty halitosis
onto my unhappy orifices,
my hands are chapped
and the clouds are
an ugly shade of
cold front purple,
floating overhead
relentless and moist,
the horses running
and the birds gone.
I am now muddy
and groaning,
stuck in the mire
and breathing ice.
Winter, why,
oh why are you here,
I'm not yet at
the date of my birth
and you have come,
your voice whispering
at corners of windows,
telling me to sleep,
while I shiver under
heavy blankets,
it tells me to
close my eyes
and feel
its cold hands
reaching for me,

for my night
to begin,
and I will
dream at last
of death.

Sleepy Highway

The sleepy sky yawns,
I drive alongside
yellow stripes,
they hum in beats
to a country song,
and I do too,
as I wait for sky
to blink her pink lashes
and shake loose
all the colors
of her crimson dress,
a gauzy affair
shook loose of stars
and the grip of
jealous yellow moon
who disappears
into an ocean,
who will be back
tomorrow night
as they all do
with their promises.
This Montana day,
this long road
is lined with
thoughts of chickens,
truckloads of hay
and winter wheat
sleeping in brown dirt,
it smells like sage
and a thousand pieces
of my past, teepee rings

that sing in the wind,
a stray coyote
returning to the den,
running late across
a grassy yellow field,
I nearly spill my tea
but continue on
and I smile,
because this is my home,
this is where I sit and wait
for my big sky to unfold
and run with colors,
every shade of lavender,
red and pink running
like beautiful blood
down the drain of evening,
and then, at dawn,
reborn as softness,
a sweet lavender ribbon
of horizon cutting
the blue land from sky,
and as the sun slowly
creakily rises into dawn,
my road ends here,
landed at last in Montana.

Something Ran Across the Road

Flowing down
into the black
tunnel of night,
a flash of gray
speckled with
prairie umber,
a flash of feral eyes,
my hand wavers
and my heart
is so afraid,
this is how it
goes, Montana
high-ways
into night,
serves up
a platter of
bloody delight,
a path of malice
for fearful travelers
who crawl along its
grass lined back
hoping not to see
something that
ran across the road,
with haunted eyes
and ribs that cage
wild hearts and hunger.
in its simplicity,
it turns around,
it watches me,
parts the grasses,
then disappears into
the portal to its soul.

Peering Into the Cracked Mirror of a Marriage

I didn't have to be there but a challenge was issued and I answered. I am a tougher stronger more loving person for what I survived and I will never regret loving him.

Nizhoni-Oh

The vagina speaks up
and they all listen,
ears perked sharply
long into night
perched and waiting
for its call,
a shout out,
a tweet,
a barrage of need,
that hearkening call,
and then,
oh then,
the thunder
of applause,
the hammering
of feet
running to
a death
on the rocky wall,
where it waits
on the other side,
sipping a cup of tea
and munching
on a handful
of yesterday's
bloody offering.

Here is your blessing today,
sunlight peering in through
dusty slatted curtains,
a perfect egg yoke,

warm and creamy,
the steam from
freshly buttered toast,
and the screen of the day
filtering in on a beam of light.
This is my Arizona,
the beady stare of
horny toads,
and the sweet sting
of red ants
on my wash day,
spiders in my socks
and sand in the holes
of my soul,
then later,
a black eye and some
green chile,
washed down with an
ice cold beer,
oh boy, get me some more,
and then let's roast the pig
out on that fire,
she's ripe and ready,
and the sunsets here
are glorious.

Desert Rain

It's raining in my kitchen,
pattering gently onto the
sincere black & white floor.
The clean linoleum counter
spared its relentless spatter;
it's raining in my kitchen
and it won't stop soon.

The desert day begins slowly,
dazzles, simmers and sizzles.
Its weary tenants plod on
to jobs or shade, whichever
they are lucky to find.
Along a dusty roadside,
a dog dies, begins to bloat,
food for the flies and birds,
a warning to survivors
to veer away, to steer clear
of the whining and whizzing
ribbons of mindless traffic.

In nearby dry gully brush,
dark skinned men talk low
and pass a brown bottle,
catcalling unseen to passersby.
Jackrabbits in greasy bush
chew their wads of cud,
waiting for the blessed green
of evening and safe darkness.

It's raining in my kitchen,

a baby girl stirs in my belly
safe from this red shower,
he stands over me with a fist,
I slipped and fell and now,
it's pouring in my kitchen and
I don't have a way out of the rain.

~~~April 1982~~~

Just Stop It

Looking at roses,
....strange....
it makes me think
of blood
slowly dripping
onto dirty
linoleum,
an old floor
in an old
stone building,
full of spiders
and cockroaches;
it is 1982
and I have your baby
squirming in my belly
like kittens in a
plastic bag
mewling for
their little lives,
drip, drip,
onto the floor
soaking into
Arizona dust,
the red rock stuff
blasted off of
nearby cliffs
onto my floor,
while my blood
drips and drips
out of my nose
that you hit,

because I washed
your jeans
that were on the floor,
that were full of
black widow spiders,
so...
I saved you
but you
killed my
love.

You Shouldn't Have

The lips were
pale antique rose,
the cheeks blushed
and soft as
the nappy neck
of a kitten,
the small hands,
fingers knitted
into each other,
nervous and alive,
and the eyes
as soft as the
dewy gaze
of a deer
trapped on the
edge of an abyss.

You were a
dangerous storm
soaring in to
knock me down,
you were the wind
I dared to swallow,
the glare of a
devil driven mad
by its own voice,
thunder and
lightening
striking long into
a vast cavernous
night.

Flowers could be
a sweet scent
or a poison
held out by
your strong hands;
I grasped gently
and placed in water,
careful to mix sugar,
a spot in the dappled
afternoon sun,
and an open door
to my bed.

You shouldn't have;
those flowers,
the possession,
your arms holding
me down,
your fist,
the shout and
the slam,
and the end of
it all,
the end of the
long tunnel,
the end of
twenty years,
the black eye,

oh God, why...
you shouldn't have,
oh why...
you shouldn't have
done that to me.

A Man in a Grave

Here we are again,
you and I, my love,
breathing in cold wind,
airborne North Dakota dirt
and blue sky spilling over
and onto your last bed.
You are asleep now,
your hands crossed
solemn and grave,
so very peaceful.
I envy your grace,
your noble expression,
the dark brown hands
that held me so tight
and that bore fists
that lay me on floors,
so easy to forget
blood and tears,
how I fell out of love
and back in again,
here at your grave
where you sleep
and I know you wept
for me like I now weep,
a thousand tears
and a million wishes,
if only I had stayed,
if only.

Divorce/Poverty

I lasted longer in that marriage than a lot of women; so many others would have run blindly into the woods after the first punch. The divorced life I entered was sometimes more troublesome than the marriage but still full of freedom and hope. The climb was ever upwards and continues to this day.

Burnt Weenies and Honey

Here we go again.
He tossed out
the weenie water,
the kittens,
all five of them,
plus my damn heart
and twenty good years,
roasted green chile
and beer scented,
a slap as good
as a punch.

In both instances,
I catapulted
to orbiting stars,
experienced yellow,
red, the feedback
vibrating hum of
reentry.

Our decaying orbit
flung me away,
you knew it did,
but trajectories
of tragedy
fly true in
skies of pain,
and in my flight away,
I think I heard you cry.

Ejaculation Nation

You rule the planet with big feet,
the loud voice coming in the door
at the end of your ugly work day.
You are pissed off and angry,
here I am in my warm kitchen
waiting for it to begin to rain,
the enemy rain with vicious eyes,
the many forms of violence,
the fist, the deep voice raised
like a sonorous foghorn leading me
onto rocks, to my utter shipwreck,
foolish salt and pepper despair,
stupid, lost and stranded,
ridicule that keeps me small,
judgment that makes me run
like a tiny rodent in a wheel
with my little feet and hands,
the judgment that follows me
with derisive superior eyes,
eventual flight into threadbare life,
the divorce, supposed freedom
that flung me into poor pockets,
sitting in government offices
waiting, watching the mail
for that little piece of money,
standing in food bank lines
in desolate winter rags,
looking at other worn shoes,
unaware of my own,
thin and dirty,
wearing a sour face and heart.

I am all alone again,
finding new forms of abuse,
the fuck buddy,
willing to hang on tight so
tenderly and with kindness,
his blue eyes watching me,
so solicitous and concerned,
looking all around to see
my poor little apartment,
the toe hole in my humble sock,
small boy in front of the TV eating
little dinner of macaroni & weenies,
this is my glamorous life here,
like what you see, mister?
The deal sealed with a kiss
and a fuck then you are gone,
until next week and the next,
a new violence that rapes my heart
and then hangs the flesh out to dry.
So yeah, let's be friends,
come and take what you need,
my love, my humble food,
a little warmth under my quilt
with my willingly warm body
that I trusted you with,
and then, yes, of course, I know,
you have to get up and leave,
such importance back home,

your big fat special life,
your special super duper duties,
your other lovely ladies,
with red lips and fresh linens,
waiting for you, big man,
to come back and lavish them
with what they are deserving of,
property and security, honor,
the man's big smelly money,
expensive shiny golden ring,
on their tiny delicate fingers,
the oh so solicitous concern
and gentlemanly behavior.
You may open their ornate doors
and go fetch for them now,
then forget my kind hands
and my aching heart back here
under the quilt waiting for you.
Lover, you said you loved me
not once but twice there,
your eyes as hot as tiger blood,
words breathless and passionate,
then turned and walked away,
leaving me here in my bed
in a rolling sea of sour tears,
self induced self pity self aware,
foolish choices relived.

So yeah, I guess it is over

and I can just let go, emote,
throw my despair to the wind,
burn the fragile decaying bridge
with all the bile I can muster,
let the anger blur the lines and
send you fleeing from me at last,
a clean break might be the best,
break it up then, after dust settles,
in comes the next big set of hands
with big feet stomping in the door,
cruel impatience and stern orders,
bullying needs that pull me down,
precious business, tender 5 minutes,
then goodbye, goodbye, goodbye.

You rule a mean blue planet,
your ejaculation is power,
your use is abuse;
into this ending, I go,
unwilling slave,
oh stupid woman,
rodent in a wheel,
loving kind heart,
all alone again,
I lie down and
in wishing to,
I do die.

A Free Love

He walks me to his car,
talks about his house
and his job.
He buys dinner,
a cheap dinner,
I order soup.
I see his new clothing
and the leather shoes,
as he sizes up my ass
and my willingness,
laboring for his attention.
Oh handsome white man,
I can see what you have
to offer a native gal like me.

He kisses me hard
as if I might get away.
He clutches me tight
in his greedy arms,
as if...
I smile and I try,
I really do,
I kiss him back,
his words of love,
cooing and churning,
the toss onto a bed,
pillows flung on the floor,
leftover paper plates and
a newspaper opened to
a crossword puzzle,
his cats watching us,

as we all wait, wait for his
imminent explosion,
he dies his tiny death
while I let go.

When it is all said and done,
he offers to drive me home
as if the icing on the cake
is being let out the door.
Don't you know
I am already free,
I am already gone?
Don't you know
I hate you?

I think there's a hole in my sock,
I can feel a toe questing around
the soft leather innards of moccasins,
My hair needs combing but
I don't care, I leave it a mess
so I can see that look of fear
in those prismed blue eyes,
the constriction of his anus
as it clutches his big fat
smelly wallet full of cash.
I discern your secret life,
the day life where you go
to see your friends
and to visit mom and dad

right around the corner
from here,
oh yes, I know...

O, how I live for the day when
I can wait for you to fall asleep
and then walk out the door.
Not being there in the morning
when you wake up with your
woody is just worth a walk home.
And yes, love is free,
my darling,
I take it from you, then
I spit on your filthy money
and walk out the door
to where my true love is,
my bitterly won freedom,
my poverty, my own life
where I chose to be,
and when you call
next Friday,
you will hear the phone
ring and ring
as I fly away
to my truly free love,
for my own pounding
wild heart.

Making a Fist

It seems as if
and it seems when
it was time
I didn't do it,
I didn't stand up,
and in falling,
I learned to lie low,
yet in adversity,
there also lies
the clenched fist
fighting it all,
the train wreck
of love,
the mistakes
of children
sent away
unready and unsteady,
but in my secrets
and in the attics
of thought
with its dustball
disguise,
I hold a steady fist
and I rail and fight
for all I hold true,
love and family,
my wandering feet
and mind,
regard for
my Creator,
and my constant flow,

my words, my wit,
where I end my day
with my fist
in its face
and I continue
my fight
for me.

Sex and Lies I Tell Myself

Marriage was never a sexual paradise and the sex itself became a cumbersome but necessary chore that I carried out dutifully. Now all of a sudden, I am a divorcee in charge of taking care of my own sexual needs and I got busy.

Furry Cup of Redemption

Mistaken identities
From my own soul,
Lovely lies told
To only myself,
Too long and clever,
To even fight,
To even figure out,
Too long told.

There is a furry cup
Of my own pouring,
I want to quench
This woman's thirst,
Desire that simmers
Stewing and salty
With reasons why,
All the reasons,
Ingredients for me,
For soup that is me.

There is a furry night
That waits impatiently
For me to curl into it,
As softly as breasts folded
Into infant's mewing lips,
As gentle as a lover's kiss,
Needing to be pulled into
Scratchy knapsack hands,
To be scratched and gnawed
To satisfaction, to sleep.

Hues

What are you wearing tonight?
I am wrapped in the color red,
Warmed by its glow,
I feel as though a ball of orange
Has nested in my chest,
my hair waterfalls down
Into a lush blue river,
And my hands are
flushed purple with you.
You release one drop of desire
On your forehead this evening,
Which journeys down onto
Your tummy, wet belly hair,
A puddle of neediness there,
You are clothed in it.
I let the red fall to the floor
In a silky tangled pool,
You see my orange glow
In all its glory,
Your eyes widen, you
Bring your desire close
It breathes in my ear
And purrs intently,
Your hands circle then
Pull my blue hair back,
You lick my purple
And taste its tang,
Most unladylike feelings
Stir and muddle
My best intentions,
I dip a finger into

Your puddle and
Lick its sweetness
Long into the night,
Where colors melt
And we bleed into
Night and its hues,
Blue,purple,red,orange.

In the Jungle of Your Mind

I had a dream....
you were naked
and hushed,
it was very warm
and I could hear
a bird singing
in a lush jungle,
the low silly trickle
of a minute waterfall,
a river of sweat
from your fever,
and a stillness
in your slow silky touch.
These dreams are green,
not brilliant green,
but a muted dark,
lush, verdant and
mossy green.
The dark green of
my dreams
smell like spice,
like a stallion's neck
after a hot August day,
and wet like the ocean
which throws a cloak
of fog over us both.
Your arms are so strong
and they pin me down,
but I don't struggle,
I lie still and watch,
I want to hide

from that light.
I cannot look away,
because my dream
is your universe,
you are lord
and master,
and I am tame
just for now,
my hair spread out
like a dark spider
on the velvet pillow
of my fractal mind rays,
and the pulse in my
belly tuned so finely
to yours.
You kiss me then,
your hungry mouth,
it wants to eat me,
I am soft chocolate pudding
that you lap upon,
and I am a cream pie
bursting with fluids,
waiting to be devoured,
as this feast of ours
winds on into the
landscape of my love,
this inner world of secrets
where we lie quietly,
wound together and

tangled in this dream,
verdant and velvet,
penetrating each other's souls
with our touch,
and feasting upon each other
until dawn.

Laundromat Thoughts

The circle is turning
in my head
in tune with
the rolling laundry,
tumbling out of my
own dirty thoughts
which need such
a cleaning up.

I'm remembering a man,
his tense edgy voice
and his eyes,
hard crystals
that stare at me
and dare me to
look away,
I don't and
I won't.

There are his two
strong broad hands
touching me here and there,
as gentle as a child,
and his kiss,
hungry devil
eating me alive,
and his arms of steel
that pin me against
his belly, his chest
where his heart
beats faster,
a war drum.

I can see feel his
hot breath on my neck
and in the cold night air,
the steam rising
from my back,
we are turning and
rolling with the tides,
awash in each other's
ebb and flow,
steam rinsed desire
and slippery as soap,
we glide to standstill
on the edge of
night's shimmering tapestry,
and then,
sleep.

The dryer glides to its end,
a laundromat kitty
lay in the sun dreaming,
her legs twitching,
I read a magazine and
try to forget him
and our sweet times,
for it all rolls to a stop
and then is folded
and put away
for the next
tumble.

Need

So much I needed back in those rough days, I needed companionship and love and sex and good food. I needed security and safety, but I was alone so I did my best.

Writing My List

I need
    very
        little.
A wan yellow ochre
circle of
       sad light.
Salt, a pinch of sugar
   a kiss,
       a slap.
The iron tang of
night.
Skewed splintered
doors.
Secretive skeletons
of spiders
Tiptoeing ghosts of
       children
Indian indigo lies
whiskey colored eyes,
life without fathers,
a mother's echo,
drums in circles
feathered.
Blue girls smiling,
polka
    dots on
        teepees,

I need
   just
      a little,

meat juiced,
roasted,
foot pounding
runs
through velvet
    highs,
flying and flying
away
dancing on
cinnamon
and fruit dotted
    red,
and landing
in the
stew of
forgiveness.

I need
    just
        a little
crazy dogfight
strung up
barbwire
and the
sting of
    freedom,
        color,
            flavor,
                flight.

For All the Rocks

The drive that takes me home is
Lined by ragged weeds, gophers
Darting across to secret dens,
As I rock and roll on by,
Thoughts planted deep in
Frozen ponds full of memories,
Rising bubbles and whispers,
Begging for attention,
And remembrance,
The road lulls me,
Humming its sweet lullaby,
Taking me home.

I hit a rock and
Propel into a more
graceful state,
I find the rocks,
All they see and do,
Their dull gray faces
To wind, rain and snow,
Bedecked with bright red
And yellow lichens,
Rubbed and well worn
By my passage.
I lumber along into
Another monotone gray day,
Approach a rock on the road, which
Sprouts legs then darts upwards,
It has grown wings and now
It flies away,
And then another,

Taking to the skies
That hang low and moan,
The skies that beg for
Just a little warmth,
For the snow to cease,
And the clouds to part,
To exhale its pale blue breath,
To give this tired land some life,
And my exhausted soul
a pair of wings.

My Cup

What does a punch and slap
taste like?
Twenty years of stifle.
And what do the tears
sound like
when they hit the ground?
Muffled and forgotten,
machine gun fire
and a torrent
of angry.
How does the open sky
feel to someone
who sees only the ground?
Where do the flawed souls
go to die?

There is said to be
a candle in a window
for all those fortunate ones,
a lovely lily scented candle
wafting its gentle fumes
onto those pretty pretties,
with their dainty fingers
their delicate filigree lives
edged with lacy perfection,
turning everything to gold
with just a pursing of
lush red lips in the direction
of their desire,
the candle guiding him home
where she lies in wait

complete in her love
and gifted in her spell.

I will sit in a dark window
and watch the rain fall,
I know there is no one
coming for me,
I have to learn to "like,"
no, not just "like,"
I have to "like like"
being alone here,
teaching a little boy
to be a man,
when I am a woman,
and not a very good one,
for all that.
There is no bread
in the oven
nor is there any longer
a fire within me
to light the candle
that will send a beacon,
a ray to the one I love.
So no, I don't have to be nice
and I don't have to like like
anything,
I just need to lie down
tired in my bed
and close the lids

where the show rages on,
the voices that pummel my
conscience,
the scenes of regret
and the vows
fervently mouthed
to not repeat.

What is a cloud
and what does it feel like?
Where is the reason
in the clear pool
of dawn,
where I bathe in
its cooling morning
and step out clean?
Where is the cup
and when may I
ever drink it again?

Sleeping Alone

Night stirs its dark inky soup
colors swirl into its broth,
quiet silky needs and desires
flowing like honey into the mix,
a sigh for a lover far away
and the memories that come
forbidden and unwanted,
I embrace the sadness,
fold my heart around
my precious grief,
as I push the sorrow away,
ruffle feathers of impatience
and then, as the stars stop
their dance to gaze at me
in the bejeweled winter night,
I remember to smile,
just let things be,
like a spider who caught a fly,
he ate up my essence
and then let me go,
so here I lie in this bed,
the decision is there in purple dark,
do I live as a withered corpse
bled of love or
shall I replenish my stores
for all who are here with me,
for those who stay by my side,
the little boy with his dark eyes
watching me always,
the kitty with her big orange eyes,
waiting for a scratch and a pat,

my girls who need twenty bucks
and some encouragement,
and the good friends with their needs,
for all that they give back to me,
I will lie here in this lonely bed
and smile and feel the true blessings
for the man who leaves me here,
in the dark night, the sorrow flows away
and dissipates in the love that is here,
and for the sheer calculated risk of
living for right now, the quiet house
that sleeps with peace and security,
the full belly, the warm clothes on my back,
and for the memories of a man
who can't be here, for all that he gave me
before we parted and flew away
from each other,
for these I smile here in the dark
and mouth a silent 'thank you'
to the Creator who watches over me
and who wishes for me
to be happy.

Who Am I? What Am I?

Typical question for any human being but especially so for me. Having lived by the strict rules of dysfunction, family, religion, marriage, I was suddenly in wide open territory as far as how I could choose to live my life. That included sculpting a personality out of a person who had her head down for so long, raising my head and looking at a completely new world and finding out who the hell I really was.

Grendel's Bride

Am I a horse's hoof?
Is it hard prairie sod
that I tread?
Am I as cruel
as Montana winter wind,
or as gentle as a mother's
sweet kiss on a sleeping
infant's downy head?
Am I a maternal leader
or a forgotten key
under a muddy doormat?
Am I a black eye and
a bloody nose,
or a bird flying far far away?

Am I ever as beautiful as
the brilliant sun glinting
through a sleepy jagged forest,
or as desperately ugly as
an orphan on a dusty backstreet
counting the day's pennies?
Am I as mean as I appear?
And why?
Is kindness a weakness I fear
more than all the love
I could reap with mere words?

The mirror is a liar and says, "No."

The mirror is a liar and says, "Yes."

Heyah

Here's what it feels like,
the thoughts running,
hammering my brain
peppering my eyes,
the pointing finger,
the accusations
how i hate myself,
how i look,
how i smell,
the dirty face
and the hair
everywhere.
This is what i do,
i take the day,
twist it around
my sweaty fist,
i take the night
and fill up my soul
with burnt spider webs
and painful liquid thoughts
that drip acid and bile
into the empty cavern
of a lost heart.
This is how it ends:
i lie down and watch
the lines crawl across
the ceiling of dreams,
i listen to the thumping bass
drown out the voices
that shout and yammer
behind my sore eyes,

watch everyone's smiles
melt into clown grimace
rigor mortis claws,
grins that bare
bloody teeth,
i go down, down
into the darkness
that holds no kindness
on this blighted evening,
and i find no peace
in the velvet crawl
into my filthy high.

Mistaken Beauty

She was flawless,
milky radiant skin
and sculpted nose,
lush curved bosoms
that begged for caress,
her golden hair
flowed down her
chiseled back
as if spun
from purest honey,
her blue eyes
were plucked
from a summer sky,
her lips cherry red
as if kissed by
strawberries with
blueberries dancing
their scent around
her clothing,
she moves smooth
and liquid
across the dreams
of his hunger,
she brings him
to arched perfection
in his lust and need.

Thus the dreams of men
unfurl onto the glossy
pages of our daily read,
we thumb idly past

these visions of
milk and honey,
we only want
to reach that impossible
pinnacle of perfection,
while our dark hair
uncoils in a tangle
down our backs
made strong by hard work,
burdened by children
and flexible with life,
our hands are torn and
worn by care as we tend
to our lives, nails cracked,
face lined with wisdom,
sadness, laughter,
eyes reddened by tears,
wind, work,
and our bodies
are carved and left
so very human,
bellies of worn muscle
that stretched with life,
and then were stripped empty,
to sag and hang sad and forlorn,
and our hearts as well,
they are filled and emptied
day by day,
as we cook, clean, work,

wipe our children's noses,
care for our homes,
rush off to work
unaware of the crumbs
we've left behind on our counters,
the shoes and dirty socks,
broken crayon on a kitchen floor,
children shooed off to their day,
and we go to ours.

Where will ever come the time
to sit and powder my nose,
to run a smoothing iron
down the tangled dark hair,
or to stop the hand of time
that has scrawled lines
across my weary face,
when will my skin ever bloom
in a blush of rose and
the brown tones of my people.
when will my hands ever be
plump and moist with youth,
and my feet agile,
my belly flat and alluring,
where is this face that is me,
staring into the mirror day after day,
this tired face tilted and curious,
the eyes still looking for what?
it's just me, no more, no less,

and i know that there must be
a little bit of beauty left
from where the young girl
stepped into her adult life,
and began her tumble down
to where i sit now,
i know it's there somewhere
in my worn and weary heart
as i march through my life,
so here is where i will
plunk my homely self down
and see the beauty that is there
for one who seeks past
the shell that a loving heart occupies
and who will see past this worn woman's
facade into her forever youthful
and her beautiful rainbow soul.

The Human in Me

I see in the mirror
above my bed
these bare breasts
dimpled in the cool
of my bedroom,
peaked in the purple
darkness,
where the lingerie
is stepped over,
a velvet pool of
shimmering black
nightie.
I see my soft belly
rise and fall
with each weary
soul breath,
I touch,
close my eyes
and I just
am a woman,
just for tonight,
where I lie
alone
in the silent bed,
a ticking clock
and the curtains
that flit and
undulate as slow
as the moon's
numbed path,
then slumber

and pass
into dreams where
I am merely human,
a touch of color,
the lips red
and the soul
so blue,
the bruises purple
and golden fade;
I drift above
in a hue,
a hum,
an invasion,
I fly above
my sincere landscape,
sewn with careless
stitches,
crazy quilt country,
where spiders watch
my every move,
the monster waits
behind a pillow,
and I fly on by
so unaware,
I sit on a cloud
and sing,
there is no body,
I am just a thought,
a feather,

pulled to the edge,
looking down,
a shapeless person
a paper bag,
arms and legs
and nothing
but me in between,
I smile and
fly into my night,
where magenta skies
and alizarin crimson
prairies full of
speckled dun horses
churn and stampede,
I fly into those skies,
here in the dream,
where I am human,
I am just the
essence
of a me.

One Legged Bird

"My shit's fucked up."
~~Warren Zevon~~

My feathers
are painted
red, alarming
and screaming,
bleeding into
rivers that
roar and pound
the shores of
moaning voices,
my feathers
are sky blue,
labor against
prairie winds,
they sweat and
float in scented
puffs of sagebrush,
they sing in the
voices that drum
and caress my ears,
the feathers rise
and form wings,
one legged bird
that I am,
for I fly well
but cannot land,
I ride over vast
grassy landscapes
but am untethered
by the dirt or rocks,

by any soul there,
looking for me,
always grasping,
but my feathers
take me away,
they reach deep
inside my soul
and fling me aloft
to strange lands
that no one else
can ever see,
I smell the ocean
and the ragged pines
of vast elder forests,
I see brown churning
herds of shaggy hearts
plying the prairie,
and watch the horses
pummel rainbows into dirt,
on their way to their home,
clouds ahead of me now,
yellow grain earth behind,
patchwork of landscape
unreeling under me,
I fly on with my feathers,
going nowhere,
never stopping,
and I never
land.

Searching for Kind Elaine

It seems
that the world
was so immense,
the coulee
where I played
was a grand canyon
of games and
silence and
thought,
a spider
was company
and anthills
were cities
full of
busy busy
commuters
on their way
to work.
the sky was
a blue giant
who formed
pure white clouds
into amusing shapes,
while we children
lay on lawns
as soft as
a kitten's belly
and saw
an entire zoo
up there.

I was silent
and watched,
I saw trouble
and tears,
I saw disagreements
and fists raining
down on
pliant flesh,
I heard the word,
no,
and I obeyed
with a mere
yes.
my hair
traveled
slowly down
my back
through the
aching misery
of years,
my eyes
watched
the unrolling
spool of this
life of mine,
as if I were not
even featured,
never a star
in my own life story,

a mere footnote,
spectator
and speck
on the
wall.
I flew
away from
reality
often,
as a child,
a teen,
an adult,
a long
lonely
journey
up and over
everything
and
every
one.

somewhere along
the way to now,
that girl got lost,
her smile,
her care,
her love,
melted away.
I want her back,

no more anger,
no more fear,
I want her to
come out and play,
to lie on soft lawns
and watch clouds
float gently by,
I want her to
feel the wind,
and love the rain
in her hair,
how it ripples
and tickles.
I want her to
smile again,
and I want her
to be kind,
as she once was,
surrounded by
sisters,
and to be
good,
so good
and kind.

Healing, Moving Ahead

I'm getting closer to my home. I've talked to people who told me to just live in the moment, not knowing what that ever meant. I've done therapy, taken pills, drank, indulged my senses. And these things could never guarantee happiness or peace of mind. I have had to work on healing all the pain and suffering, all the years of silence and depression. And I've made a breakthrough, I have seen the other side. It's electric, terrifying, amazing, it is the now we seek and there is no looking back anymore.

Letting Go

Sometimes,
I can see right
Through to
The other side
Of what appears
To be a wall,
Which becomes a
Thin wavering nothing,
Fragrances that vaporize,
Magnetic, electric, fragile,
And then, the feeling
That I don't care,
A sensation of falling
And not looking down,
A dust mote thought
The notching of an arrow,
A flight to the bullseye,
And there I can just exist,
Happily unaware of anchors
Of fear, of bodily intrusion,
The harnesses of the skin,
I can merely just be,
Like a flower's scent
That never apologizes,
A sweet sound that
Undulates and lands
In someone else's ears,
An aimless drifting
Of snow across bare land,
Or water on endless stretches
Of empty eggshell beaches,

That I am merely the sound
Of wind tickling a wind chime,
Awakening the sky to shades
Of crimson or lavender,
Sending missiles of pink
Into blue canvas heights,
Or I might just be a cloud,
Formless and stupid,
Floating above it all,
Never speaking of what I see.
And maybe this is merely
What it all is,
A careless drive through
The countryside of our lives,
And the vehicle that we inhabit,
The reckless chariot of our minds
Lurching down rock strewn roads,
Maybe then, we will slow
Our pacing nervous journey
As sweet pastures of peace
Draw closer, watch a tree
Sitting alone afield, see a bird
Alight there and wait for us,
Perhaps then, we will stop,
Get out and lie in the grasses
That wait to cushion our fall,
While all else slowly winds
Down and
Stops.

My Comfort Zone

My comfort zone
is out beyond
the walls
of safety,
past serene
pastures
and grazing
beasts,
beyond
sunlight
and a
bright silver
moon,
long past
civil grace,
teacups,
the mall,
a schoolyard;
I'm so far gone
that I can't
see anything
but a prairie
dust storm
and a pale
blue Montana
sky,
I smell
a Chinook
wind
full of snow
and look

into shiny
pools of
a deer's
dark eyes,
staring
down life's
doorway,
an eagle's
song across
mournful purple
mountains
and sad umber
fields of silence;
that's where
I exist,
that is where
I wander,
but comfort
is a zone,
comfort is
no voices
or faces
or eyes,
comfort is
solitude
and silence,
my comfort
is there
where my soul

got left behind
before it was
buried and lost
to love and life,
jobs, bills,
children,
and when
I go to lie down
and reach out
for silver light
of a winter moon
that has slithered
into a hole in
the curtain,
lingering on
my pillow,
maybe then,
I find my comfort,
my zone
in silent
unassuming
moon
light.

Remembering to Forget

There is so much
I have forgotten,
idle here on this
squeaking swing,
listening to the
busy fall wind,
the paper rustle
of burgundy, gold
and tinseled leaves
wobbling to the ground,
where they blanket
and close off my thoughts.
I feel a glimmer,
and I remember...
no, I won't...
it's best to forget
and let autumn
do its work,
to deaden and silence
an already tepid heart
and bring me to rest
in time for a thick
white silent blanket
of snowy cold,
for my heart to slumber
in a den of safety,
hoary with frost
and icicles of
past events,
a hand that remembers
its haphazard journey

across your belly,
in a quiet warm bed,
the war of a heart
wanting to fly
but lying in wait,
a tangle of souls,
deep velvet sleep.
So here I sit
in my autumn swing,
alone in an abandoned playground,
the solemn squeak of the chain,
wind that chatters around my feet
slows to an indolent whisper,
and in its gentle sway
I am lulled and,
for just a second,
I forget and I watch the skies
and see the colors of leaves,
I dig into my heart
to squeeze the feelings out,
in amazement at my life,
allow my soul to embrace
and maybe to love
the gentle pain of past losses,
to acknowledge my present life,
and all its goodness,
and I forget
for just a second,
all the sorrow of loving,

I forget about you,
so far away,
and I forget
to hurt.

The Fiber of a Day

I wake up late,
gray seeping in
on my dreams,
those rainbow wishes
wilting away into
winter's calling,
a ship sailing away,
its distant port
of call on
the other side
of my day.

Today,
I will water my plants
sweet pea green fronds
curling around my fingers,
so fresh and inviting,
gulping at the water,
like hungry children
around a garden hose
on a wilting august day.

Today,
I will wash my hair,
cascade of gray and ash brown,
a river flowing down,
so soft,
its gentle waves
caressing
the lines of my
muscled back,
the edges curling around

the strumpet tattoo,
and ticking my bottom
gently as I
run a comb through
its stubborn tangle.

This afternoon,
I will window shop
and look at shoes,
admire the stitch and weave,
the domain of women,
our wonderful obsession,
the sexy red high heels
that I wish to conquer,
the sensible loafer
that I eventually surrender to,
the funny purple converse
high tops
that rule my Saturday,
and the wonderful warm
furred snow boots.

This evening,
I will take this food,
break this bread,
soft and warm from the oven
and let the yeasty odors
mingle with the
buttery moment,
a touch of honey

just right,
a crunchy carrot,
and the sweet bite
of cinnamon,
a family well fed
and loved.

Tonight,
I will sit with them,
the child
and the silly cat
and laugh
into the evening,
our bellies full
and our hearts
nested and content;
I am close again
to my dreams,
those secrets
that no one dare ask,
the unfurling tapestry
of the soul,
uncovered and scrolling
on into the wee hours
where impatient stars
burn out exhausted
into the eventual
gray dawn of
another winter day.

Coming Home to You

Seems as if he's been there waiting for me forever. Why did I wait so long, why was I such a wild animal that could not see that the door has been wide open? But no mind, I'm here now and I'm home at last.

A Love Note Left Under Your Pillow

You sleep as though
the night were a plow,
it has mowed me down
and left me drowning
in your seed,
I am restless and
at bloody dawn,
arise to bloodshot skies
and hot confused pillows.

You sleep as though
the dawn were a pill,
it has drugged me
senseless to your kiss
that left bruises to fade
and fists to wave,
I am hungry and
your austere kitchen
offers nothing.

You sleep as though
the kitchen were kittens
seeking mother's milk,
and my stomach
mewls for kindness.
Daylight watches me
silently searching,
while you sleep as though
I were still there,
and as the door clicks shut
your hand finds a crumpled note
I left under your pillow.

Nightmare Repairs

I awaken with
an air-gulping
liquid sob,
warm bedroom,
rumpled blankets,
afloat in sadness.
The dream buzzes
back before me.
You stood before me,
you had a finger
on a sore spot,
I cried out,
Oww, OWW,
Stop it.
STOP IT.
You smiled
and you
did
not
stop.

I dream of my
kitty kat,
she's an old
lady of 15 or 16.
Thin, sleeping a lot,
losing teeth and hair.
Her thin haunches
and hollow belly,
never full,
never satisfied,

yet I feed her
and feed her.
She is hungry
once again
and I am angry.
But as I look at her face,
her eyes,
and as I bend down
to kiss her whiskered cheek,
the doctor pushes
a needle in and ends her life.

The bedroom air has grown cold,
I refuse to cry although
my throat is thick with despair.
What is the analogy here
that will end this feeling of betrayal?
Am I the kitty kat?
Am I an old lady in a young man's arms?
Will my life end at his hands
as he bends to kiss my cheek?

Rivers continue to push,
mountains pull.
I smell berries there.
The snap of a bow
behind a tree
brings me to my knees.
I look down and see

red snow blossoms.
Somewhere else
an airplane carries
burdens across the skies,
and burps up life onto
highways pumping and
throbbing.

You awake at dawn
and rise,
I am now reaching out,
and the nightmare
repairs begin.

The Usual Path

The snowy plateau
That gives way to
Cloudy heights,
The gradual climb
And the journey
Across mountains,
Slumbering slobs
Drenched in white caps,
Sleeping with
Soft blankets of fog,
Showering in sun,
A glimpse of a frothing
Line of white rimmed river,
Spewing its madness onto
Miles of green shoreline
on down into churning falls,
As I close my eyes
And open them to
A city crazy with cars
And sunlight and heat,
People rushing about
As if it would matter,
As if it ever could,
I rush to the curb
To wait, and then
I see you coming,
I see your smile
And the journey
Begins and then
The journey
Ends.

This Is How It Began, This Is How It Ends

These are but drips of poetry from a flood of writing in the past 15 years, but it chronicles a journey to self awareness for this little beast of a woman that I am. No apologies, no regrets, not afraid to look back and chuckle at it all. I hope you enjoyed this crazy journey, there was a gush and outpouring of poetry during these troublesome years but oh so many gifts that were set before me. And it brings me back to that silly little poem about sunflowers, teacups, sugar cubes that I wrote not so long ago. This is my simple truth. There are more poems to write, more books to compile, more life to cherish.

Thank you.

Sugar for My Soul

Is what I really need
In my own two hands?
Can I learn to look in the mirror
And to walk out the door strong
like a man?

I don't want to peek around corners
For the rest of my life
I don't want to be nice all the time
But I will have a cup of tea
Every single day
And I will take two lumps
of sugar for my soul.

Elaine S. Gerard

Elaine was born in Browning, Montana, as a member of the Blackfeet Indian Nation. She grew up in a small Montana prairie town and was educated at the Institute of American Indian Arts, Santa Fe, New Mexico, and the University of Montana, Missoula, Montana, graduating with a degree in fine arts, Native American studies and business education. She has lived in Montana, Nebraska, Arizona, New Mexico, Oregon and Washington and now resides in Spokane, Washington, with her partner and his daughter. She writes extensively and enjoys photography, sewing, acrylic painting, beadwork and spending time with family.

grateful acknowledgement is paid to the journals that previously published the following poems:

"Sugar for my soul," *Bellowing Ark*, May/June 2006

"Don't eat the snow," "Blue Horses" and "Reading Tracks," *Haight Ashbury Literary Journal*, Volume 34, Number 1

"Paying the Cultural Rent," "One Legged Bird," *Yellow Medicine Review*, Fall, 2017

"Grendel's Bride," *Nomad's Choir*, Fall, 2019 issue

www.ingramcontent.com/pod-product-compliance
Lightning Source LLC
Chambersburg PA
CBHW052140110526
44591CB00012B/1800